MARGAM DEPOT

MARTIN BRAY

AMBERLEY

I would like to dedicate this book to all the staff in South Wales
that helped, encouraged and made it happen for me.
Thank you.

First published 2021

Amberley Publishing
The Hill, Stroud
Gloucestershire, GL5 4EP

www.amberley-books.com

Copyright © Martin Bray, 2021

The right of Martin Bray to be identified as
the Author of this work has been asserted in
accordance with the Copyrights, Designs and
Patents Act 1988.

ISBN 978 1 3981 0372 6 (print)
ISBN 978 1 3981 0373 3 (ebook)

British Library Cataloguing in Publication Data.
A catalogue record for this book is available from
the British Library.

Origination by Amberley Publishing.
Printed in the UK.

Introduction

Margam Servicing Depot was built on a landfill site and opened during March 1964. Its function was to service locomotives operating to and from Margam Knuckle Yard, which was acclaimed as being the most highly mechanised in the United Kingdom.

With the opening of Margam Depot, Duffryn Yard was closed and its allocation of Class 08 shunting locomotives – D3429–D3438 – were transferred to it. Although no mainline locomotives have ever been allocated to Margam Depot, most classes have visited it for servicing.

During March 1976, British Steel opened their new iron ore terminal in Port Talbot Docks and Margam Depot was responsible for providing traction for what became an iconic train of three Class 37 locomotives hauling twenty-seven 100-ton iron ore tipplers from Port Talbot Docks to Llanwern steelworks. In its time it was one of the heaviest freight trains to run on British Rail, requiring strengthened couplers, and attained a maximum speed of 8 mph at the top of Stormy Bank.

With the decline in the 1980s of oil, coal and steel traffic in South Wales, Swansea Eastern, Llanelli, Pantyffynnon and Landore depots closed and the work was transferred to Margam Depot.

In July 1996, Margam Depot became part of the privatised company of English, Welsh and Scottish Railways (EWS).

A further decline in freight, mail and parcels traffic saw the restructuring of EWS, resulting in the closure of Canton Depot in May 2004 and the transferring of thirty fitters to Margam Depot. As a result of this the depot was extended, and a 2.5-ton overhead crane was installed to facilitate locomotive examinations and component changes.

Due to over capacity at Toton Traction Maintenance Depot, Margam Depot temporarily carried out 'B' exams on Class 60 locomotives and undertook investigative and remedial work on rogue locomotives.

During September 2008, extensive flooding took out the power supply to the depot and due to the high cost of a replacement cable, a 200 kVA mobile diesel generator was brought in.

With the continuing contraction of EWS's maintenance requirements, Margam Depot was officially closed on 1 August 2009. However, a second power unit change was required on a Class 08 shunting locomotive and the depot finally closed on 17 September 2009, with some staff transferring to Margam Knuckle Yard.

The closure of Margam Depot has left South Wales with very basic servicing facilities, with all other work being transferred to Toton Traction Maintenance Depot.

This book is a pictorial history of the many types of locomotives that have been serviced by Margam Depot since its opening, together with the transition of liveries from British Rail green through Railfreight grey to EWS burgundy.

No. 08367, formerly D3437, was built by British Rail at Crewe Works in June 1958 and was one of a batch of seven shunting locomotives (D3432–D3438) that was transferred from Duffryn Yard to the newly opened depot in 1964. It is depicted in British Rail blue livery on 18 June 1983 and was scrapped at Gwent Demolition during March 1994.

No. 08368, formerly D3438, was built by British Rail at Crewe Works in June 1958, scrapped at Swindon Works during October 1984 and is depicted in British Rail blue on 26 May 1980 while undergoing maintenance.

No. 08466 *Brillo*, formerly D3581, was built by British Rail at Crewe Works during October 1958, scrapped by CF Booth and is depicted in EWS livery on 18 March 2007. No. 08466 was unofficially named *Brillo* after a retired painter at Canton Depot who used Brillo pads for his painting preparation work.

No. 08466 *Brillo*, formerly D3581, was built by British Rail at Crewe Works in October 1958, scrapped by CF Booth and is depicted in EWS livery on 7 April 2007.

No. 08493, formerly D3608, was built by British Rail at Doncaster Works in February 1958, scrapped at CF Booth during August 2008 and is depicted in British Rail blue livery on 23 March 1997.

Accident-damaged No. 08587, formerly D3754 was built by British Rail at Crewe Works in September 1959, scrapped at TJ Thompson during December 2009 and is depicted in EWS livery on 20 January 2007.

No. 08630 Bob Brown, formerly D3797 was built by British Rail at Derby Works in November 1959 and is depicted in EWS livery shortly after its naming ceremony, celebrating the life of Bob Brown at Margam Depot on 14 March 2008. Bob Brown was a former Margam Depot driver that passed away while on duty. No. 08630 is owned by GBRF, numbered Celsa 3 and is named *Celsa Endeavour*.

No. 08646, formerly D3813, was built by British Rail at Horwich Works in February 1959, scrapped at EMR Kingsbury during November 2015 and is depicted in Trainload Freight livery on 8 March 2008.

No. 08662, formerly D3829, was built by British Rail at Horwich Works during May 1959, scrapped at TJ Thompson during September 2012 and is depicted in EWS livery on 27 November 2005.

No. 08752, formerly D3920, was built by British Rail at Crewe Works during December 1960 and is depicted in EWS livery while undergoing its second power unit change with the generator from withdrawn No. 09003 *Tattoo* on 30 July 2009. The reconditioned generator that was used in the first power unit change was found to be defective. The power unit change was undertaken by depot staff using the Cowans Sheldon 75-ton breakdown crane. No. 08752 is owned by Rail Support Services.

The power unit, including the original generator from No. 09003 *Tattoo*, is being lowered into No. 08752 on 30 July 2009.

No. 08770 *Benny*, formerly D3938, was built by British Rail at Crewe Works during March 1960, scrapped by TJ Thompson and is depicted in Departmental grey livery with coal sector decals. No. 08770 was unofficially named *Benny* after a retired fitter's assistant at Canton Depot and was being cannibalised for spare parts due to a defective power unit on 24 May 2009.

No. 08782 *Castleton Works*, formerly D3950, was built by British Rail at Derby Works during April 1960. It is owned by the Harry Needle Railroad Company and is depicted in Corus livery on 6 May 2007. The locomotive has been fitted with remote-control equipment and flashing lights for one-man operation in Celsa Works, Cardiff.

No. 08854 *Bradshaw*, formerly D4022, was built by British Rail at Horwich Works during June 1960 and No. 09020, formerly D4108, was built by British Rail at Horwich Works during November 1961. Both are depicted in EWS livery. No. 08854 was unofficially named *Bradshaw* after a retired fitter at Canton Depot and scrapped at EMR Kingsbury during May 2012 while No. 09020 was scrapped at EMR Kingsbury during February 2012.

Nos 08900, 09102 *Hento* and 09011 *Gully* are all depicted in Departmental grey livery on 31 July 2005 and withdrawn from service. No. 08900, formerly D4130, was built by British Rail at Horwich Works during May 1962 and scrapped at TJ Thompson during February 2009. No. 09102, formerly D4000 and No. 08832, was built by British Rail at Derby Works in October 1960 and scrapped at EMR Kingsbury during November 2011. No. 09011, formerly D4099, was built by British Rail at Horwich Works during September 1961 and scrapped at EMR Kingsbury during November 2011. Nos 09102 and 09011 were unofficially named *Hento* and *Gully* after a retired fitter and fitter's assistant at Canton Depot.

No. 08941 *Viv*, formerly D4171, was built by British Rail at Darlington Works during June 1962, scrapped by CF Booth and is depicted in EWS livery on 7 August 2005. No. 08941 was unofficially named *Viv* after a retired fitter at Canton Depot.

No. 08951 *Fred*, formerly D4181, was built by British Rail at Darlington Works during
September 1962, scrapped by CF Booth during December 2011 and is depicted in EWS livery on
24 January 2009. No. 08951 was unofficially named *Fred* after a retired fitter at Canton Depot.

No. 08957, formerly D4191, was built by British Rail at Darlington Works during August
1962 and scrapped by Harry Needle Railroad Company during February 2004. It is depicted
in almost ex-works EWS livery on 10 August 1997 and was withdrawn from service due to an
incident at Onllwyn Washery that shifted its cranks and twisted its frame.

No. 08994 *Gwendraeth*, formerly D3577 and No. 08462, was built by British Rail at Crewe Works during August 1958, owned by Harry Needle Railroad Company and is depicted in EWS livery on 22 April 2000 with cut-down cab for working on the former Burry Port & Gwendraeth Valley Railway.

No. 09003 *Tattoo*, formerly D3667, was built by British Rail at Darlington Works during February 1959, scrapped at EMR Kingsbury during September 2011 and is depicted in EWS livery receiving the scrap power unit from No. 08752 on 30 July 2009. No. 09003 was unofficially named *Tattoo* after a retired fitter's assistant at Canton Depot.

No. 09003 *Tattoo* after donating its power unit to No. 08752 on 16 July 2009.

No. 09020, formerly D4108, was built by British Rail at Horwich Works during November 1961, scrapped at EMR Kingsbury during February 2012 and is depicted in EWS livery. No. 09105, formerly D4003 and No. 08835, was built by British Rail at Derby Works during November 1960, scrapped at CF Booth during February 2011 and is depicted in Departmental grey livery on 13 April 2008.

No. 09102 *Hento* is depicted in Departmental grey livery and was being cannibalised for spare parts on 17 April 2006.

Nos 20168 and 20059, formerly D8168 and D8059, were built by English Electric at Vulcan Foundry during October 1968, and Robert Stephenson and Hawthorns during May 1961 respectively. No. 20168 is depicted in British Rail blue livery while No. 20059 is depicted in the original Railfreight grey livery with a red solebar and were both being kept in warm storage for future preservation on 14 May 2000. No. 20168 is owned by Harry Needle Railroad Company while No. 20059 is privately owned.

No. 20904, formerly D8041 and No. 20041, was built by English Electric at Vulcan Foundry during November 1959 and is owned by Harry Needle Railroad Company. It is depicted in Hunslet Barclay livery top and tailing No. 20901 on a Nomix-Chipman weed-killing train on 9 April 1989.

No. 37012, formerly D6712, was built by English Electric at Vulcan Foundry during March 1961 and scrapped by Simms Metals during August 2003. It is depicted in British Rail large logo blue livery on 22 April 1990.

No. 37042, formerly D6742, was built by English Electric at Vulcan Foundry during June 1962. It is privately owned and is depicted in Trainload Freight Metals sector livery on 27 March 1993. This livery was worn by locomotives moving steel and iron ore trains around the various steelworks and end users.

No. 37043, formerly D6743, was built by English Electric at Vulcan Foundry during June 1962, scrapped at McIntyre during May 2003 and is depicted in Civil Engineers livery with Transrail decals on 23 May 1999. This livery was worn by locomotives carrying out railway infrastructure work.

No. 37078, formerly D6778, was built by English Electric at Robert Stephenson & Hawthorns during October 1962, scrapped by EMR Kingsbury during February 2004 and is depicted in British Rail blue livery on 27 March 1989.

No. 37078, formerly D6778, was built by English Electric at Robert Stephenson & Hawthorns during October 1962, scrapped by EMR Kingsbury during February 2004 and is depicted in Trainload Freight Petroleum sector livery on 21 May 1990. This livery was worn by locomotives moving oil, diesel, petrol and chemical trains around the various refineries to oil terminals and end users.

No. 37087, formerly D6787, was built by English Electric at Robert Stephenson & Hawthorns during December 1962, scrapped by CF Booth during March 2012 and is depicted in Civil Engineers livery with black numerals on 9 July 1995.

No. 37108, formerly D6808, was built by English Electric at Vulcan Foundry during January 1963, is privately owned and is depicted in Trainload Freight livery on 21 April 1996. This livery superseded the British Rail blue livery.

No. 37139, formerly D6839, was built by English Electric at Vulcan Foundry during May 1963, scrapped by TJ Thomson during February 2004 and is depicted in British Rail blue livery on 11 February 1989.

No. 37145, formerly D6845, was built by English Electric at Vulcan Foundry during May 1963, scrapped by Raxstar and is depicted in Trainload Freight Metals sector livery on 10 February 1991.

No. 37158, formerly D6858, was built by English Electric at Vulcan Foundry during August 1963, scrapped by Harry Needle Railroading Company during April 2008 and is depicted in British Rail blue livery on 25 February 1990.

No. 37189, formerly D6889, was built by English Electric at Robert Stephenson & Hawthorns during January 1964, scrapped by TJ Thomson during December 2010 and is depicted in British Rail blue livery on 26 May 1980.

No. 37212, formerly D6912, was built by English Electric at Vulcan Foundry during January 1964, scrapped at Eastleigh during January 2004 and is depicted in Transrail livery on 24 May 1997. Transrail, Mainline and Load Haul were three regionally split freight companies that were set up to replace Trainload Freight operations in 1994.

No. 37215, formerly D6915, was built by English Electric at Vulcan Foundry during January 1964 and is privately owned by the Growler Group. It is depicted in Trainload Freight Petroleum livery on 31 March 1991.

No. 37221, formerly D6921, was built by English Electric at Vulcan Foundry during January 1964, scrapped by CF Booth in May 2009 and is depicted in British Rail blue livery on 4 March 1989.

No. 37222, formerly D6922, was built by English Electric at Vulcan Foundry during January 1964, scrapped by TJ Thomson during August 2008 and is depicted in Trainload Freight Coal sector livery on 9 May 1993. This livery was worn by locomotives moving industrial and household coal, and nuclear fuel trains.

No. 37223, formerly D6923, was built by English Electric at Vulcan Foundry during February 1964, scrapped by Sims Metal during April 2003 and is depicted in Trainload Freight Coal sector livery on 9 May 1993.

No. 37248, formerly D6948, was built by English Electric at Vulcan Foundry during October 1964, is privately owned by the Growler Group and is depicted in Trainload Freight Petroleum sector livery on 3 March 1991.

No. 37293, formerly D6993, was built by English Electric at Vulcan Foundry during July 1965, scrapped by CF Booth during February 2009 and is depicted in Trainload Freight Metals sector livery on 27 March 1993.

No. 37350, formerly D6700 and No. 37119, was built by English Electric at Vulcan Foundry during December 1960, is owned by the National Railway Museum and has been repainted back into British Rail green livery on 16 June 1991.

No. 37371, formerly D6847 and No. 37147, was built by English Electric at Vulcan Foundry during June 1963, scrapped at Wigan CRDC during June 2001 and is depicted in the original Railfreight grey livery with a red solebar on 21 March 1992.

No. 37375, formerly D6893 and No. 37193, was built by English Electric at Vulcan Foundry during February 1964, scrapped by EMR Kingsbury during January 2008 and is depicted in Mainline livery without decals on 27 May 2000. Mainline is one of the three regionally split freight companies that were set up to replace Trainload Freight operations in 1994.

Nos 37401 and 37426, formerly D6968 and D6999 and Nos 37268 and 37299, were both built by English Electric at Vulcan Foundry during February 1965 and August 1965 respectively and are both depicted in EWS livery on 27 May 2000. These are both waiting to take a steel train from Port Talbot steelworks to Llanwern steelworks via the Central Wales line due to engineering work on the Great Western mainline. At this time heavier locomotives that would normally work this train were not permitted to work over the Central Wales line. Wisconsin Central purchased Transrail, Load Haul and Mainline freight companies and formed them into EWS (English, Welsh and Scottish) railways in 1995. No. 37401 is owned by DRS while No. 37426 was scrapped at CF Booth during March 2013.

No. 37402, formerly D6974 and No. 37274, was built by English Electric at Vulcan Foundry during April 1965, is owned by DRS and is depicted being repainted into an unofficial and revised Trainload Freight livery on 1 June 2003. The former Managing Director of Valley Lines railway, where this locomotive was being operated, was not too impressed with the livery and dubbed it 'mushroom soup' livery.

No. 37403, formerly D6607 and No. 37307, was built by English Electric at Vulcan Foundry during October 1965, is privately owned by the Scottish Railway Preservation Society and is depicted withdrawn from service in Brunswick green livery on 8 March 2008.

No. 37408 *Loch Rannoch*, formerly D6989 and No. 37289, was built by English Electric at Vulcan Foundry during June 1965, scrapped at EMR Kingsbury during January 2008 and is depicted in EWS livery waiting for some minor accident damage to be repaired on 3 July 2005.

No. 37411 *Castell Caerffili* and No. 37425 *Pride of the Valleys* have been repainted into green and large logo British Rail blue liveries respectively on 31 March 2007.

No. 37411 *Castell Caerffili*, formerly D6990 and No. 37290, was built by English Electric at Vulcan Foundry during June 1965, scrapped at CF Booth during May 2013, has been repainted into green livery and is pictured on 14 May 2005.

No. 37413, formerly D6976 and No. 37276, was built by English Electric at Vulcan Foundry during April 1965, scrapped at CF Booth during April 2017 and is depicted in EWS livery on 11 October 2008 and withdrawn from service.

No. 37415, formerly D6977 and No. 37277, was built by English Electric at Vulcan Foundry during April 1965, scrapped at CF Booth during November 2013 is depicted in EWS livery on 31 May 2008 and withdrawn from service.

No. 37419, formerly D6991 and No. 37291, was built by English Electric at Vulcan Foundry during April 1965 and is owned by Direct Rail Services. It is depicted in EWS livery on 7 August 2005 and is being prepared for reinstatement to service following the withdrawal of accident-damaged No. 37408.

No. 37419, formerly D6991 and No. 37291, was built by English Electric at Vulcan Foundry during June 1965, is owned by Direct Rail Services and was brought out of store and repainted in to EWS livery on 9 August 2005 following the withdrawal of No. 37408 due to accident damage at Rhymney.

No. 37422 *Cardiff Canton*, formerly D6966 and No. 37266, was built by English Electric at Vulcan Foundry during February 1965, is owned by Direct Rail Services and is depicted in EWS livery on 16 February 2003. This locomotive was the first of three to be given F exams at Canton Depot for Valley Lines passenger work in 2002.

No. 37425 *Pride of the Valleys*, formerly D6992 and No. 37292, was built by English Electric at Vulcan Foundry during July 1965, is owned by Direct rail Services and is depicted in large logo British Rail blue livery awaiting maintenance on 21 October 2006.

No. 37427 *Bont Y Bermo*, formerly D6988 and No. 37288, was built by English Electric at Vulcan Foundry during June 1965, scrapped at CF Booth during February 2013 and is depicted in large logo British Rail blue livery on 16 July 1989.

No. 37428, formerly D6981 and No. 37281, was built by English Electric at Vulcan Foundry during May 1965, scrapped at CF Booth during March 2013 and is depicted in Royal Scotsman livery on 19 March 2005. No. 37428 wore this livery for working the Royal Scotsman train in Scotland.

No. 37668, formerly D6957 and No. 37257, was built by English Electric at Vulcan Foundry during January 1965, is owned by West Coast Railway and is depicted in Trainload Freight Petroleum sector livery on 27 March 1993.

No. 37669, formerly D6829 and No. 37129, was built by English Electric at Vulcan Foundry during March 1963, is owned by West Coast Railway and is depicted in EWS livery heading a line of stored locomotives on 29 April 2006.

No. 37675 *Margam TMD*, formerly D6864 and No. 37164, was built by English Electric at Robert Stephenson & Hawthorns during August 1963 and is depicted in Transrail livery on 17 February 2001. No. 37675 was part of the Sandite fleet of locomotives for autumn but was scrapped by EMR Kingsbury during October 2010.

No. 37689, formerly D6895 and No. 37195, was built by English Electric at Robert Stephenson & Hawthorns during March 1964, scrapped at EMR Kingsbury during March 2011 and is depicted in Trainload Freight Coal sector livery on 15 July 1990.

No. 37691, formerly D6879, No. 37179 and latterly No. 37612, was built by English Electric at Robert Stephenson & Hawthorns during October 1963. It is owned by Harry Needle Railroad Company and is depicted in Railfreight grey livery on 12 May 1990.

No. 37693 *Sir William Arrol*, formerly D6910 and No. 37210, was built by English Electric at Vulcan Foundry during November 1963, scrapped by EMR Attercliffe during May 2011 and is depicted in Trainload Freight Coal sector livery on 15 July 1990.

No. 37694, formerly D6892 and No. 37192, was built by English Electric at Robert Stephenson & Hawthorns during February 1964, scrapped at EMR Kingsbury during January 2008 and is depicted in Trainload Freight Coal sector livery on 15 July 1990.

No. 37695, formerly D6857 and No. 37157, was built by English Electric at Vulcan Foundry during July 1963, scrapped at Hull of Rotherham during April 2008 and is depicted in original large logo Railfreight grey livery on 3 April 1988.

No. 37697, formerly D6943 and No. 37243, was built by English Electric at Vulcan Foundry during September 1964, scrapped at CF Booth during March 2006 and is depicted in Trainload Freight Coal sector livery on 9 May 1993.

No. 37698, formerly D6946 and No. 37246, was built by English Electric at Vulcan Foundry during October 1964, scrapped at CF Booth during January 2010 and is depicted in Load Haul livery on 12 October 2008. Load Haul was one of the three regionally split freight companies that were set up to replace Trainload Freight operations in 1994.

No. 37704, formerly D6734 and No. 37034 was built by English Electric at Vulcan Foundry during March 1962, scrapped at TJ Thompson during June 2009 is depicted in EWS livery heading a line of stored Class 37, 47 and 56 locomotives on 19 March 2005.

No. 37798, formerly D6706 and No. 37006, was built by English Electric at Vulcan Foundry during January 1961 and was scrapped by CF Booth during July 2009. It is depicted in Mainline Freight livery on 16 June 2007.

No. 37883, formerly D6876 and No. 37176, was built by English Electric at Vulcan Foundry during October 1963, scrapped in Spain following completion of its contract hire and is depicted in Trainload Freight Metals sector livery on 24 September 1989.

No. 37888, formerly D6835 and No. 37135, was built by English Electric at Vulcan Foundry during April 1963, scrapped at Puig Vert is Spain after working construction trains and is depicted in Trainload Freight livery on 27 April 1997.

No. 37890, formerly D6868 and No. 37168, was built by English Electric at Robert Stephenson & Hawthorns during October 1963, scrapped by Rod Hull during August 2010 and is depicted in Trainload Petroleum sector livery on 9 March 1993.

No. 37896, formerly D6931 and No. 37231, was built by English Electric at Vulcan Foundry during March 1964 and scrapped at Hull during August 2010. No. 37896 is depicted in Transrail livery and sandwiched between two snow ploughs on 26 December 2004 in preparation for snow clearance. The two snow ploughs have been converted from steam engine tenders.

No. 37898, formerly D6886 and No. 37186, was built by English Electric at Robert Stephenson & Hawthorns during November 1963, scrapped at EMR Kingsbury during November 2011 and is depicted in Transrail livery on 20 November 2004.

No. 47002, formerly D1522, was built by Brush during June 1963, scrapped by CF Booth during June 1994 and is depicted in British Rail blue livery on 11 February 1989.

No. 47070, formerly D1654 and more latterly Nos 47620, 47835 and 47799, was built by British Rail at Crewe Works during January 1965. It is privately owned and is depicted in British Rail blue livery on 15 June 1983.

No. 47087 *Cyclops*, formerly D1673 and latterly No. 47624, was built by Brush during April 1965, scrapped by CF Booth during September 2006 and is depicted in British Rail blue livery on 14 March 1981.

No. 47094, formerly D1680, was built by British Rail at Crewe Works during May 1965 and scrapped by MC Metals during December 1994. It is depicted in Trainload Freight Petroleum sector livery on 28 December 1988.

No. 47112, formerly D1700, was built by Brush during January 1964 and scrapped by MRJ Phillips at Old Oak Common Depot during May 1997. It is depicted in Railfreight grey livery on 4 March 1989.

No. 47142 *The Sapper*, formerly D1735, was built by Brush during May 1964, scrapped by Vic Berry during September 1999 and is depicted in Railfreight grey livery with a red solebar on 16 June 1991.

No. 47150, formerly D1743, was built by Brush during June 1964, scrapped at TJ Thompson and is depicted in Trainload Freight Petroleum sector livery on 27 May 1989.

No. 47190 *Pectinidae*, formerly D1840, was built by Brush during June 1965, scrapped by CF Booth in April 1998 and is depicted in Trainload Freight Petroleum sector livery on 24 June 1990. No. 47190 was originally allocated to the Stanlow oil pool for servicing Ellesmere Port oil refinery.

No. 47197, formerly D1847, was built by British Rail at Crewe Works during June 1965, scrapped by TJ Thompson during January 2008 and is depicted in Trainload Freight Petroleum sector livery on 16 April 1990.

No. 47237, formerly D1914, was built By Brush during November 1965, is owned by West Coast Railways and is depicted in Railfreight grey livery on 11 March 1990.

No. 47238 *Bescot Yard*, formerly D1915, was built by Brush during December 1965, scrapped by Harry Needle Railroad Company during December 2001 and is depicted in Trainload Freight Distribution livery on 11 March 1990.

No. 47284, formerly D1986, was built by British Rail at Crewe Works during January 1966, scrapped by EWS during November 1999 and is depicted in British Rail blue livery on 10 September 1989.

No. 47309 *Ford - The Halewood Transmission*, formerly D1790, was built by Brush during December 1964, scrapped by TJ Thompson during February 2009 and is depicted in the old Railfreight Distribution livery on 21 March 1992. Railfreight Distribution was set up to move non-Trainload Freight operations as opposed to Trainload Freight coal, metals, petroleum and aggregates.

No. 47347, formerly D1828 and more latterly re-engineered into No. 57004, was built by Brush during March 1965, is owned by West Coast Railways and is depicted in Trainload Freight Metals sector livery on 10 December 1989.

No. 47365, formerly D1884, was built by Brush during July 1965, scrapped by CF Booth in October 2007 and is depicted in Trainload Railfreight Distribution livery on 16 March 2003.

No. 47375 *Tinsley Traction Depot - Quality Approved*, formerly D1894, was built by Brush during December 1965 and is depicted in the old Railfreight Distribution livery on 8 April 1990. No. 47375 is owned by Nemesis Rail and was exported to Hungary during October 2005 for further use.

No. 47377, formerly D1896, was built by Brush during September 1965, scrapped by R. Garrett at Basford Hall, Crewe, during September 2003 and is depicted in the old Railfreight Distribution livery on 16 July 1989.

No. 47452 *Ayecliffe*, formerly D1569, was built by British Rail at Crewe Works during March 1964, scrapped by MRJ Phillips at Old Oak Common during April 1997 and is depicted in large logo British Rail blue livery on 18 November 1990. No. 47452 was one of many Tinsley Depot locomotives that were unofficially named.

No. 47620 *Windsor Castle*, formerly D1654 and No. 47070, was built by British Rail at Crewe Works during January 1965 and is depicted preparing to undertake royal train duties in the original British Rail Inter City livery, devoid of decals, on 19 April 1989. No. 47620 was renumbered '47835' and more recently '47799' to became one of the two royal locomotives in May 1995. It is privately owned.

No. 47762, formerly D1768, No. 47173 and No. 47573, was built by Brush during October 1964, scrapped by CF Booth during October 2005 and is depicted in Rail Express Systems livery on 18 April 1998. Rail Express Systems was formed alongside Trainload and non-Trainload Freight operations to move mail and parcels traffic.

No. 47772, formerly D1657, No. 47073 and No. 47537, was built by British Rail at Crewe Works during January 1965, is owned by the West Coast Railway and is depicted in Rail Express Systems livery on 2 June 2007.

No. 47793 *Saint Augustine*, formerly D1778, No. 47183 and No. 47579, was built by Brush during October 1964, is privately owned and is depicted in Rail Express Systems livery on 18 April 1998.

No. 56003 was built by Electroputere in Romania during February 1977 and is depicted in Load Haul livery on 14 March 1999. No. 56003 has since been renumbered '56312' and is owned by GBRF.

No. 56004 was built by Electroputere in Romania during February 1977, scrapped by CF Booth during July 2006 and is depicted on 25 January 1998 in its original British Rail blue livery.

No. 56010 was built by Electroputere in Romania during July 1977, scrapped by CF Booth during April 2004 and is depicted in Transrail livery on 30 March 1997.

No. 56032 *Sir de Morgannwg - County of South Glamorgan* was built by British Rail at Doncaster Works during July 1977. It is owned by GBRF and is depicted in Trainload Freight Metals sector livery on 16 June 1991.

No. 56034 *Castell Ogwr - Ogmore Castle* was built by British Rail at Doncaster Works during August 1977, scrapped by CF Booth during November 2007 and is depicted in Load Haul livery on 7 March 1999.

No. 56047 was built by British Rail at Doncaster Works during July 1978, is owned by Harry Needle Railroad Company and is depicted in Civil Engineers livery with Transrail decals on 2 August 1998.

No. 56049 was built by British Rail at Doncaster Works during October 1978, is owned by Colas Rail and is depicted in Civil Engineers livery with Transrail decals on 13 September 1998.

No. 56052 *The Cardiff Rod Mill* was built by British Rail at Doncaster Works during December 1978, scrapped by CF Booth during April 2009 and is depicted in Transrail livery on 24 May 1997.

No. 56054 *British Steel Llanwern* was built by British Rail at Doncaster Works during January 1979 and is depicted in Transrail livery on 27 April 1996.

No. 56062 was built by British Rail at Doncaster Works during August 1979, scrapped by EMR Kingsbury and is depicted in EWS livery on 12 October 2008.

No. 56067 was built by
British Rail at Doncaster
Works during December 1979,
scrapped by TJ Thompson
during July 2011 and is
depicted in EWS livery on
23 June 2001.

No. 56073 *Tremorfa
Steelworks* was built by
British Rail at Doncaster
Works during February 1980,
scrapped by EMR Kingsbury
and is depicted in Transrail
livery on 8 March 1998.

No. 56077 *Thorpe Marsh
Power Station* was built by
British Rail at Doncaster
Works during May 1980,
scrapped by EMR Kingsbury
and is depicted in Trainload
Freight Coal sector livery on
3 March 1991.

No. 56090 was built by British Rail at Doncaster Works during March 1981, scrapped by EMR Kingsbury and is depicted in Trainload Freight Coal sector livery on 21 April 1991.

No. 56096 was built by British Rail at Doncaster Works during September 1981, scrapped by EMR Kingsbury and is depicted in Trainload Freight Coal sector livery on 3 March 1991.

No. 56097 was built by British Rail at Doncaster Works during October 1981, is privately owned and is depicted in Trainload Freight Metals sector livery on 18 April 1999.

No. 56099 *Fiddlers Ferry Power Station* was built by British Rail at Doncaster Works during November 1981, scrapped at EMR Attercliffe and is depicted in Transrail livery on 2 August 1998.

No. 56100 was built by British Rail at Doncaster Works during November 1981, scrapped by EMR Kingsbury and is depicted in Load Haul livery on 16 August 1998.

No. 56103 *Stora* was built by British Rail at Doncaster Works during December 1981, is owned by DC Rail and is depicted in EWS livery on 28 September 1997.

No. 56111 was built by British Rail at Doncaster Works during October 1982, scrapped by EMR Hartlepool and is depicted in its original large logo British Rail blue livery on 28 January 1990.

No. 56115 was built by British Rail at Doncaster Works during January 1983 and is depicted in Transrail livery on 10 August 1997. No. 56115 has been exported to Hungary for further use with Floyd Zrt.

No. 56116 was built by British Rail at Doncaster Works during March 1983, scrapped by EMR Kingsbury and is depicted in Load Haul livery on 26 February 1996.

No. 60001 *The Railway Observer*, formerly named *Steadfast*, was built by Brush during August 1991 and is depicted in EWS livery on 19 March 2005.

No. 60002 *High Peak*, formerly named *Capability Brown*, was built by Brush during December 1992, is owned by GBRF and is depicted in EWS livery on 9 April 2005.

No. 60005 *BP Gas Avonmouth*, formerly named Skiddaw, was built by Brush during April 1991 and is depicted in EWS livery on 23 August 2008.

No. 60005 *Skiddaw* was built by Brush during April 1991 and is depicted in Transrail livery on 25 August 1997.

No. 60007, formerly named *Robert Adam*, was built by Brush during February 1992 and is depicted in Load Haul livery with EWS decals on 17 April 2006. When EWS purchased locomotives from the three regionally split freight companies they tended to apply decals to their original livery as opposed to repainting them into EWS livery.

No. 60010 *Pumlumon Plynlimon* was built by Brush during January 1991 and is depicted in Railfreight Construction sector livery on 28 April 1991. Locomotives in this livery were used to move aggregate trains, and there were no workings for them in South Wales. However, locomotives moved from one Trainload Freight sector operator to another as workload dictated and on this occasion the locomotive was working for the Petroleum sector.

No. 60013 *Robert Boyle* was built by Brush during January 1993 and is depicted in Trainload Freight livery with EWS decals on 28 April 1991.

No. 60014 *Alexander Flemming* was built by Brush during January 1993, was the first Class 60 to arrive at Margam for crew training and is depicted in Trainload Freight Petroleum sector livery on 24 June 1990.

No. 60015 *Bow Fell* was built by Brush during March 1993 and is depicted in Trainload Freight grey livery with EWS decals on 22 July 2006.

No. 60016 *Rail Magazine*, formerly named *Langdale Pikes*, was built by Brush during February 1993 and is depicted in EWS livery on 1 June 2003.

No. 60017 *Shotton Works Centenary Year 1996*, formerly named *Arenig Fawr*, was built by Brush during October 1990 and is depicted in EWS livery on 26 July 2008.

No. 60021 *Star of the East*, formerly named *Pen-Y-Gent*, was built by Brush during December 1991, is owned by GBRF and is depicted in EWS livery with Petroleum sector decals on 16 June 2009.

No. 60026, formerly named *William Caxton*, was built by Brush during December 1990, is owned by GBRF and is depicted in EWS livery on 6 September 2009. The pipe attached to the loco is supplying air to tools being used to remove the power unit from No. 08752, as the power cable was severed to Margam Depot.

No. 60028 *John Flamsteed* was built by Brush during November 1990, is owned by DC Rail and is depicted in Railfreight grey with EWS decals on 22 April 2006.

No. 60033 *Tees Steel Express*, formerly named *Anthony Ashley Cooper*, was built by Brush during February 1991 and is depicted in Corus livery on 28 August 2005.

No. 60034, formerly named *Carnedd Llewelyn*, was built by Brush during December 1990 and is depicted in Trainload Freight livery with EWS decals on 10 May 2008.

No. 60040 *The Territorial Army Centenary*, formerly named *Brecon Beacons*, was built by Brush during February 1992 and is depicted in army livery on 16 November 2008.

No. 60042 *The Hundred of Hoo*, formerly named *Dunkery Beacon*, was built by Brush during May 1991 and is depicted in EWS livery on 26 December 2007.

No. 60044, formerly named *Ailsa Craig*, was built by Brush during July 1991 and is depicted in Mainline livery on 20 January 2007.

No. 60046 *William Wilberforce* was built by Brush during April 1991, is owned by DC Rail and is depicted in Trainload Freight livery with EWS decals on 28 April 2007.

No. 60048 *Eastern*, formerly named *Saddleback*, was built by Brush during April 1991 and is depicted in EWS livery on 1 September 2007.

No. 60049, formerly named *Scafell*, was built by Brush during May 1991 and is depicted in EWS livery on 25 January 2003.

No. 60052 *Glofa Twr - Last Deep Mine in South Wales - Tower Colliery*, formerly named *Goat Fell*, was built by Brush during May 1991 and is depicted in EWS livery on 24 May 2008. This locomotive, like others in the class, has been adorned with an unofficial Margam Depot vinyl sticker.

No. 60054 *Charles Babbage* was built by Brush during May 1991 and is depicted in Trainload Freight Petroleum sector livery on 24 March 2007.

No. 60056 *William Beveridge* was built by Brush during May 1991 and is depicted in Transrail livery on 2 March 2003.

No. 60056 *William Beveridge* was built by Brush during May 1991 and is depicted in Transrail livery on 23 August 2003.

No. 60061, formerly named *Alexander Graham Bell*, was built by Brush during June 1991 and is depicted in Transrail livery on 25 June 2009.

No. 60062, formerly named *Samuel Johnson*, was built by Brush during June 1991 and is depicted in EWS livery on 10 October 2008.

No. 60065 *Spirit of Jaguar*, formerly named *Kinder Low*, was built by Brush during September 1991 and is depicted in EWS livery on 13 September 2008.

No. 60067 *James Clerk-Maxwell* was built by Brush during September 1991 and is depicted in Trainload Freight livery with EWS decals heading a line of stored Class 60 locomotives on 1 January 2007.

No. 60068 *Charles Darwin* was built by Brush during October 1991 and is depicted in Trainload Freight livery with EWS decals on 5 April 2008.

No. 60070 *John Loudon McAdam* was built by Brush during October 1991 and is depicted in Trainload Freight livery with Load Haul decals on 13 March 2004.

No. 60074 *Teenage Spirit*, formerly *Braeriach*, was built by Brush during November 1991 and is depicted in Teenager Cancer Trust blue livery on 3 May 2009.

No. 60074 *Teenage Spirit*, formerly named *Braeriach*, was built by Brush during November 1991 and is depicted in Teenage Cancer Trust blue livery on 7 June 2008.

No. 60075, formerly named *Liathach*, was built by Brush during December 1991 and is depicted in EWS livery on 3 May 2008.

No. 60076, formerly named *Suilven*, was built by Brush during November 1991 and is depicted in Trainload Freight livery with Mainline decals on 29 May 2005.

No. 60081 *Isambard Kingdom Brunel*, formerly named *Bleaklow Hill*, was built by Brush during December 1991 and is depicted in GWR green livery on 10 August 2003.

No. 60085 *Mini – Pride of Oxford* was built by Brush during December 1991, is owned by GB Railfreight and depicted in EWS livery on 21 February 2009.

No. 60087 *Barry Needham*, formerly named *Slioch*, was built by Brush during December 1991 and is depicted in EWS livery on 21 May 2005.

No. 60091 *An Teallach* was built by Brush during February 1992 and is depicted in Trainload Freight livery with both EWS and Coal sector decals on 14 April 2006.

No. 60091 *An Teallach* was built by Brush during February 1992 and is depicted in Trainload Freight livery with both EWS and Coal sector decals on 15 December 2007.

No. 60092 *Reginald Munns* was built by Brush during January 1992 and is depicted in Trainload Freight livery with EWS decals on 24 March 2007.

No. 60095, formerly named *Crib Goch*, was built by Brush during March 1992 and is depicted in Trainload Freight livery on 27 May 2000.

No. 60099 *Ben More Assynt* was built by Brush during January 1992 and is depicted in Trainload Freight livery with Mainline decals on 9 April 2005.

No. 60100 *Pride of Acton*, formerly *Boar of Badenoch*, was built by Brush in December 1992 and is depicted in EWS livery on 13 June 2004.

No. 60500 *Rail Magazine*, formerly No. 60016 *Langdale Pikes*, was built by Brush during February 1993 and is depicted in EWS livery on 28 July 2007.

No. 66043 was built by EMD in Canada and arrived in the UK during December 1998. It is depicted in EWS livery on 8 March 2008. A total of 250 Class 66s were purchased from America to support Ed Burkhart's vision of a threefold increase in freight traffic in ten years.

No. 66077 was built by EMD in Canada, arrived in the UK during February 1999 and is depicted in EWS livery on 21 March 2009.

No. 66080 was built by EMD in Canada, arrived in the UK during February 1999 and is depicted in EWS livery on 6 September 2008.

No. 66238 was built by EMD in Canada, arrived in the UK during May 2000 and is depicted in EWS livery on 2 June 2007.

No. 67006 was built by Alstom in Spain, arrived in the UK during late 1999 and is depicted in EWS livery on 14 July 2002.

No. 67021 was built by Alstom in Spain and arrived in the UK during early 2000. It is depicted in EWS livery on 5 April 2003.

Steam locomotive Nos 76079 and 45407 are taking on water before working an excursion on 26 April 2008.

A line up of stored Class 37 locomotives on 1 January 2007.

Cowans Sheldon 75-ton breakdown crane on 31 May 2008. The crane and crew were based at Margam Depot and would attend any incident throughout Great Britain.

No. 60040 *The Territorial Army Centenary* in army livery and No. 60096 in EWS livery being serviced on 16 November 2008.

Sunset over Margam Depot on 14 February 1998.

No. 60040 *The Territorial Army Centenary* in army livery and No. 60096 in EWS livery being serviced inside the depot on 16 November 2008.

A view of Margam Depot taken from the road crossing at the west end of the depot on 3 August 2003.

A view of Margam Depot
taken further along the line
from the road crossing on 1
September 2007.

A view of Margam Depot
taken from the road crossing
at the west end of the depot on
5 April 2003.

A view looking between and through the buffers of Class
09, 60 and 66 locomotives on 5 October 1997.

Margam Depot was flooded on 6 September 2008, which resulted in the power supply being severed. A 200 kVA diesel-powered generator was hired to provide electricity to the depot thereafter.

The shunter bay was being extended on 7 March 2004 to accommodate additional work following the closure of Canton Depot.

A view Margam Depot taken from the road crossing at the west end of the depot after dark on 14 February 1998.

Margam Depot had been demolished when this picture was taken on 15 January 2012.

Margam Depot by night on 15 December 2007.

Class 60s awaiting their next turn of duty on 23 January 2005.

Class 66s being serviced in Margam Depot during the evening of 28 June 2008.

A view of Margam Depot taken from the embankment at the north side of the depot on 31 March 2007.

A quiet and empty Margam Depot on 21 March 2009.

About the Author

My interest in railways started at the age of six when my father used to drop me off on his way to work at the level crossing near Bognor Regis railway station. My passion for railways led me into an engineering apprenticeship in 1973 with one of the most respected manufacturers of railway locomotives, Ruston Diesels Limited. I had spotted all of the British Railways locomotives in the old Ian Allan pocket book by 1976, and photographed them all by 1985. I qualified as a chartered engineer in 1987 and was headhunted to South Wales in 1989, which was the start of a very close relationship with staff at Canton and Margam depots, which still continues today despite both facilities having long closed. My retirement in December 2019 has enabled me to spend more time photographing the decline of locomotives in France and landscape photography in the Canary Islands.